POP PIANO HITS

SIMPLE ARRANGEMENTS FOR STUDENTS OF ALL AGES

Girls Like You, Happy Now & More Hot Singles

ISBN 978-1-5400-3783-1

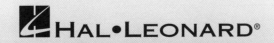

Visit Hal Leonard Online at
www.halleonard.com

Contact Us:
Hal Leonard
7777 West Bluemound Road
Milwaukee, WI 53213
Email: info@halleonard.com

In Europe contact:
Hal Leonard Europe Limited
42 Wigmore Street
Marylebone, London, W1U 2RN
Email: info@halleonardeurope.com

In Australia contact:
Hal Leonard Australia Pty. Ltd.
4 Lentara Court
Cheltenham, Victoria, 3192 Australia
Email: info@halleonard.com.au

GIRLS LIKE YOU

Words and Music by ADAM LEVINE,
BRITTANY HAZZARD, JASON EVIGAN
and HENRY WALTER

Moderately fast half-time beat

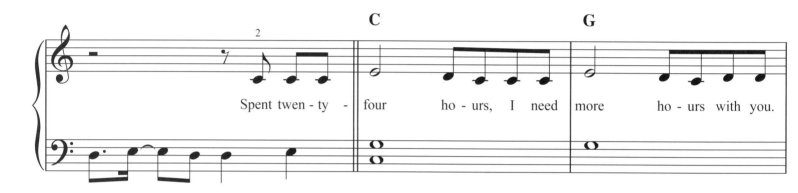

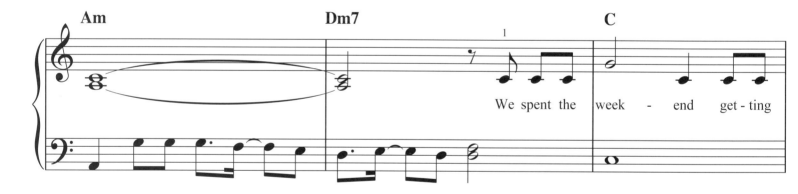

3

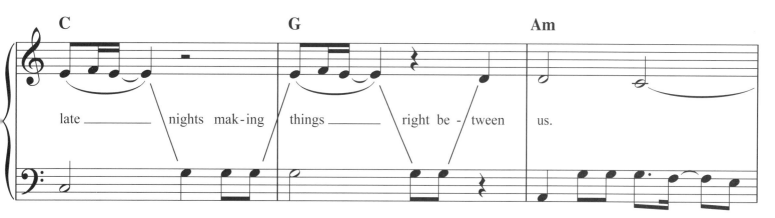

late _____ nights mak-ing things _____ right be - /tween us.

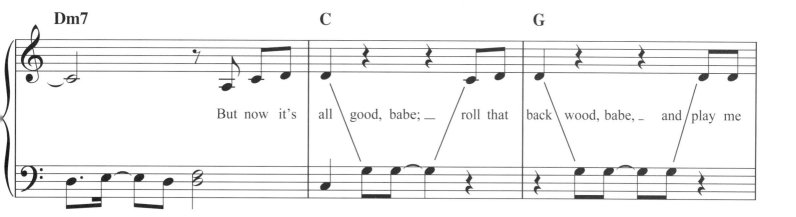

But now it's all good, babe; __ roll that back wood, babe, _ and play me

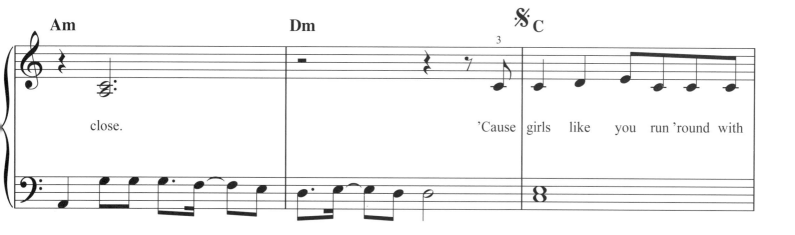

close. 'Cause girls like you run 'round with

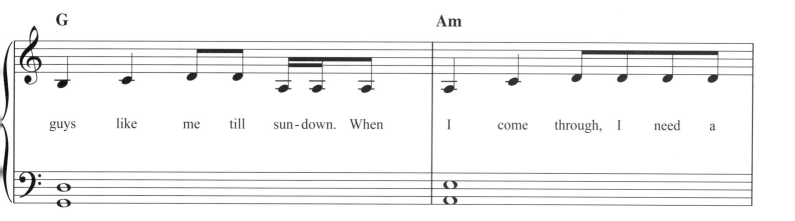

guys like me till sun-down. When I come through, I need a

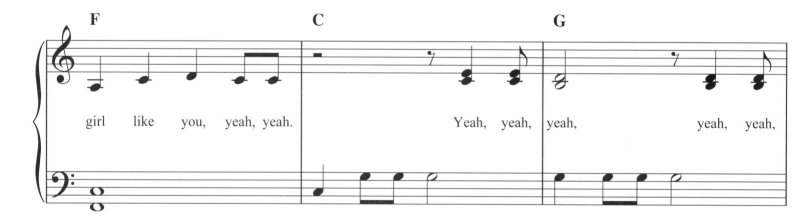

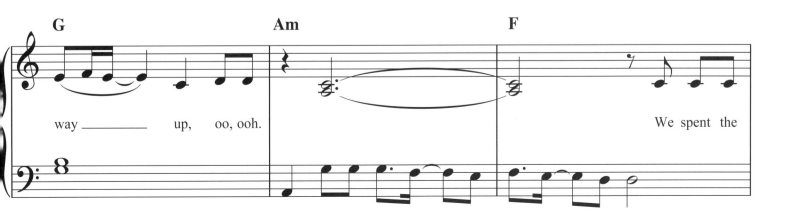

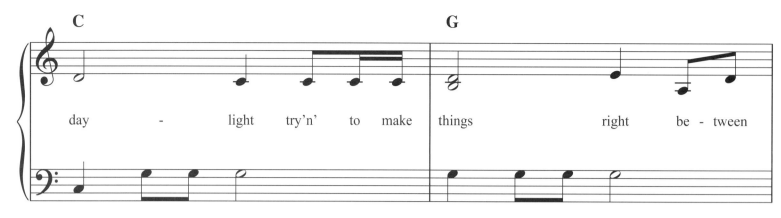

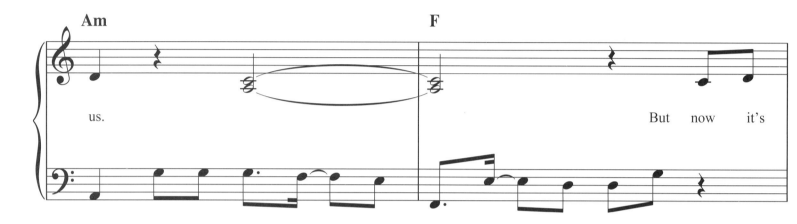

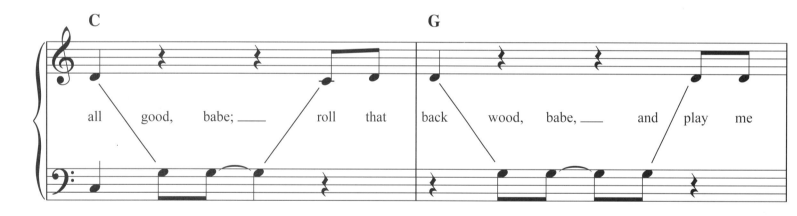

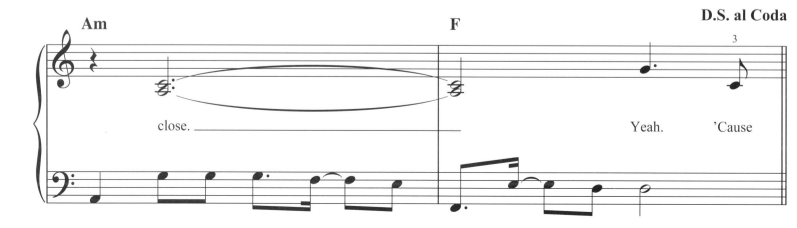

CODA

girl   like   you,   yeah,   yeah.

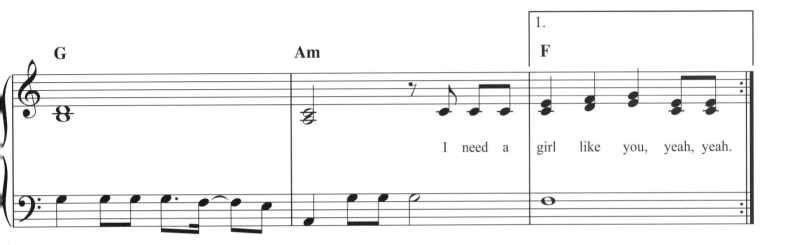

I   need   a   girl   like   you,   yeah, yeah.

girl   like   you.

HAPPY NOW

Words and Music by NOONIE BAO,
SARAH AARONS, ANTON ZASLAVSKI
and LINUS WIKLUND

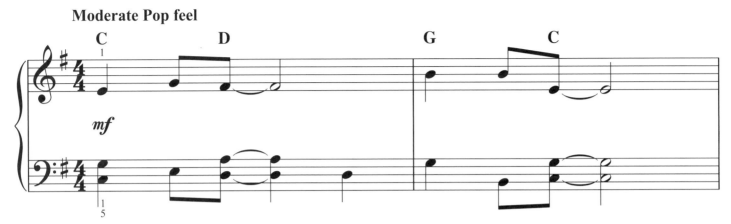

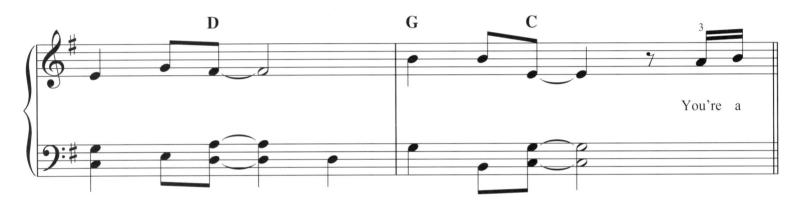

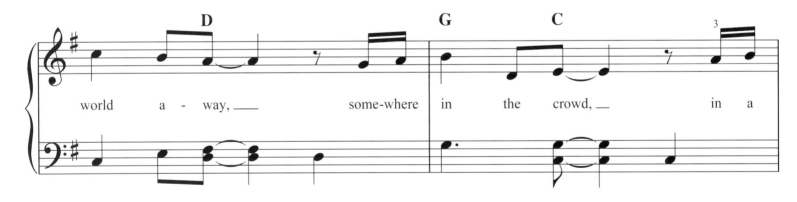

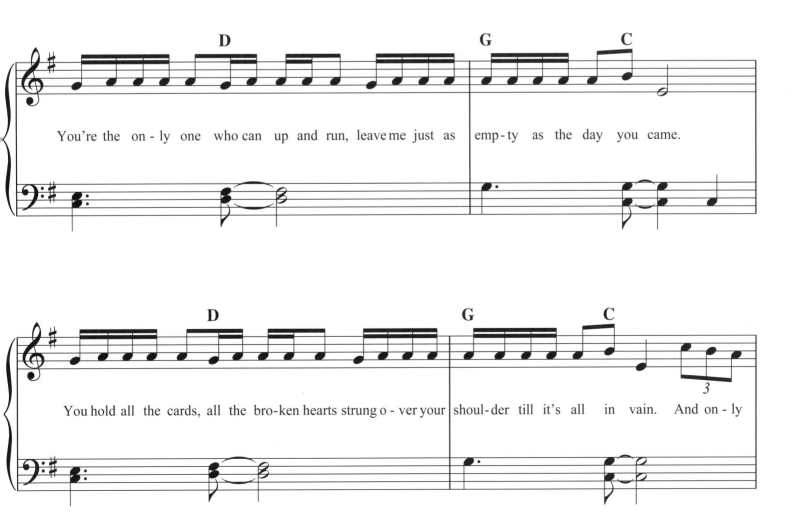

you know the strength of your teeth, the wash in the weight of your pock - ets so deep, ___

and lone - ly. You're a world a - way, ___ some-where

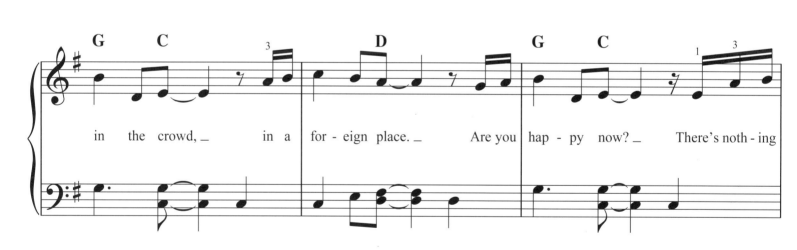

in the crowd, ___ in a for - eign place. ___ Are you hap - py now? ___ There's noth - ing

left to say, ___ so I shut my mouth. ___ So, won't you tell me, babe: ___ are you

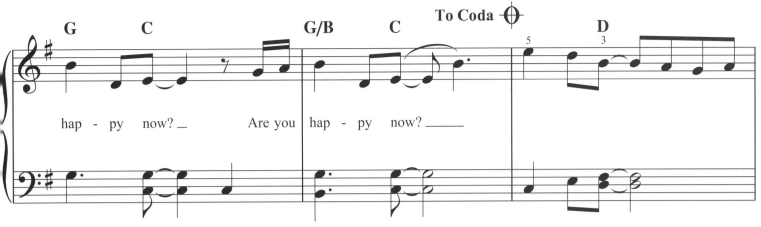

hap - py now? _____ Are you hap - py now? _____

In

the palm of your hands you can make me dance, spin me 'round in cir-cles till I'm wrapped in string. You

keep on talk-ing sweet till your fin-gers bleed, but don't you dare ask me how I've been. Now on - ly

World a - way, _ some-where in the crowd, _ in a

for - eign place. _ Are you hap - py now? _ There's noth-ing left to say, _ so I

shut my mouth. _ So, won't you tell me, babe: _ are you hap - py now? _

TREAT MYSELF

Words and Music by MEGHAN TRAINOR,
TOBIAS JESSO, ANDREW WELLS
and RYAN TRAINOR

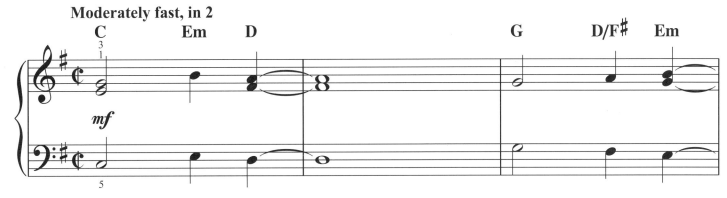

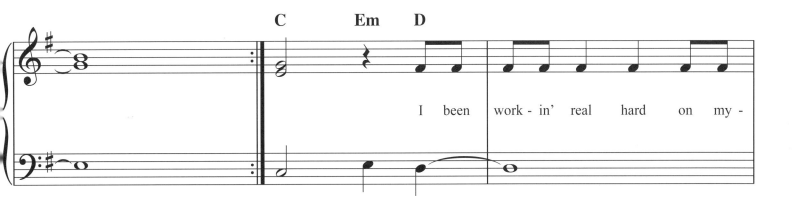

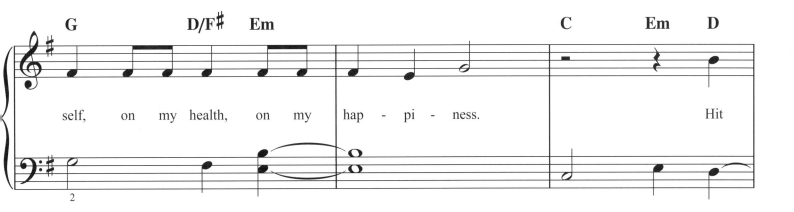

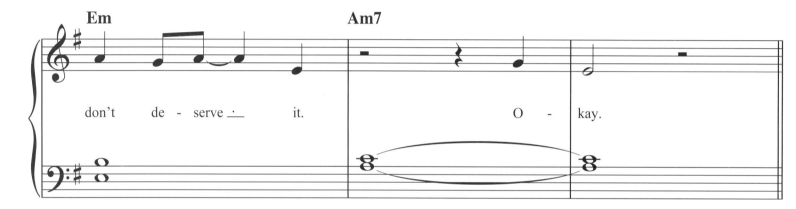

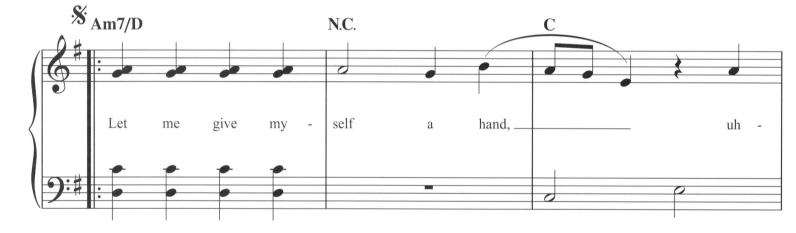

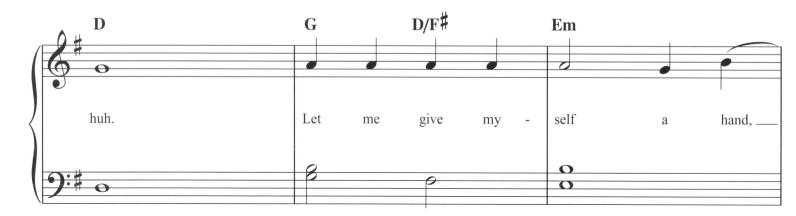

15

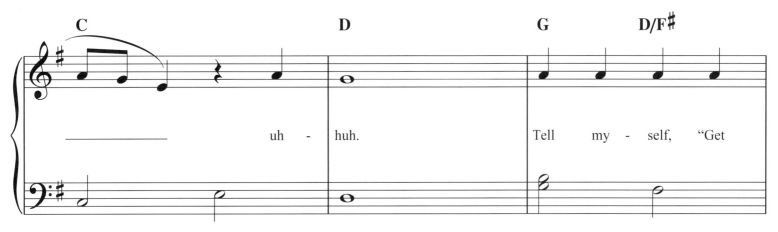

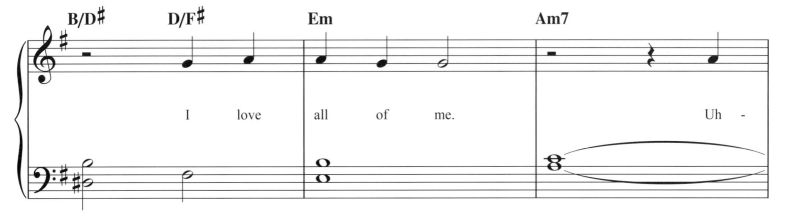

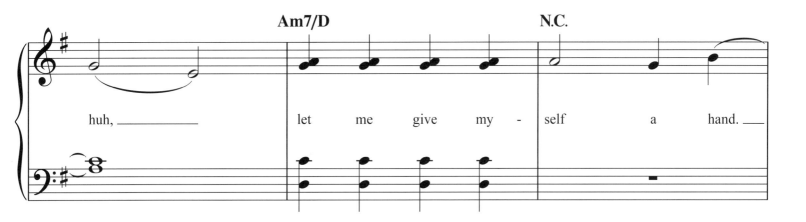

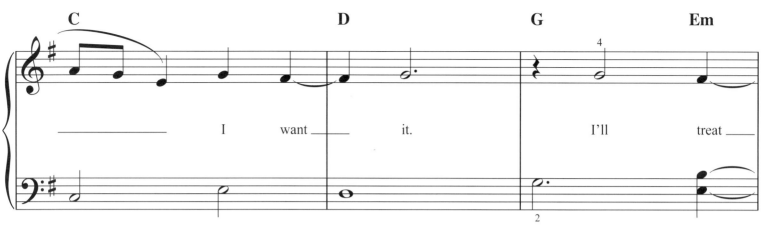

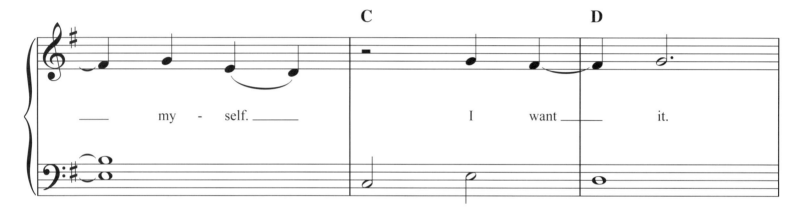

To Coda
Am7
Am7/D
Uh - huh,
let me give my...
1.
N.C.
C
Em
D
Ooh.
Ooh,
I
G
D/F♯
Em
C
Em
prom - ise to my - self that I'm - a treat me right.
Ooh,
D
G
D/F♯
Em
I'll try my best to nev - er have a sleep - less

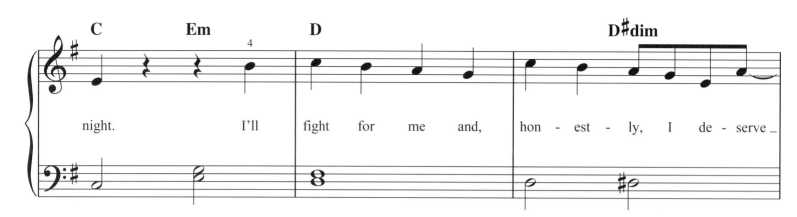

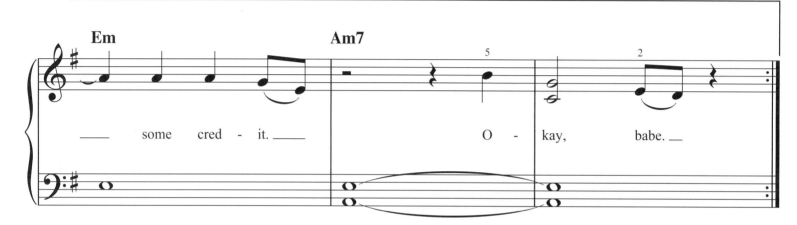

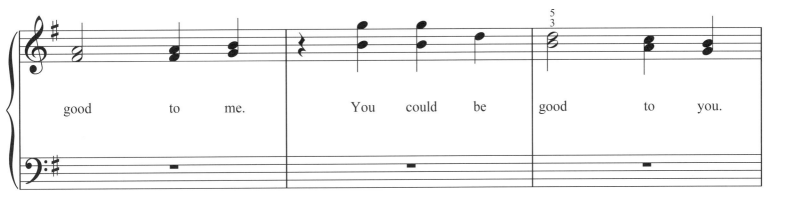

good to me. You could be good to you.

G   **D/F♯**   **G**

I'm gon' be good to me. You could be

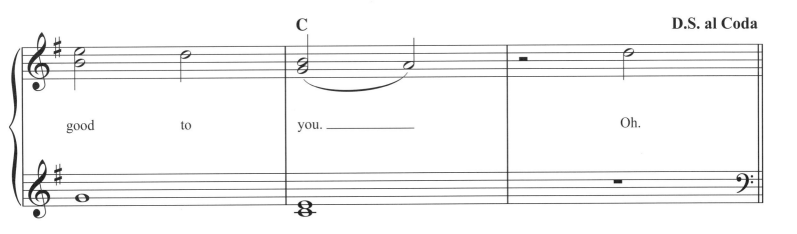

C   **D.S. al Coda**

good to you. _____ Oh.

CODA   **Am7/D**   **N.C.**

you could be good to you.

YOU ARE THE REASON

Words and Music by CALUM SCOTT,
COREY SANDERS and JONATHAN MAGUIRE

There goes my heart beat - ing,

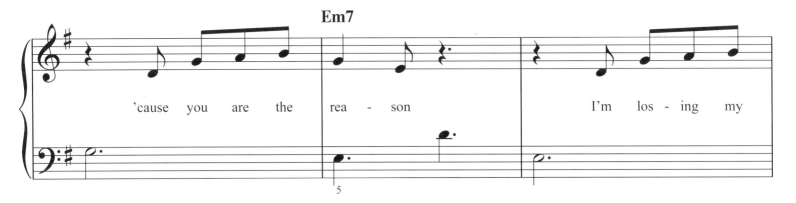

'cause you are the rea - son   I'm los - ing my

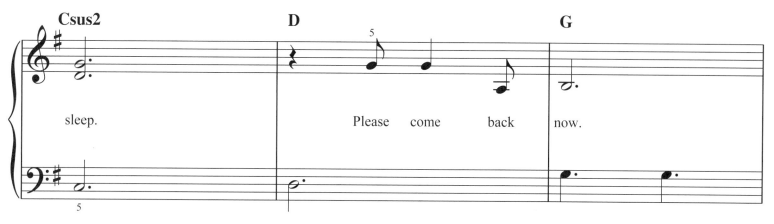

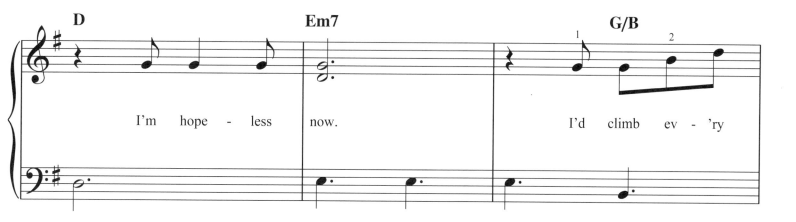

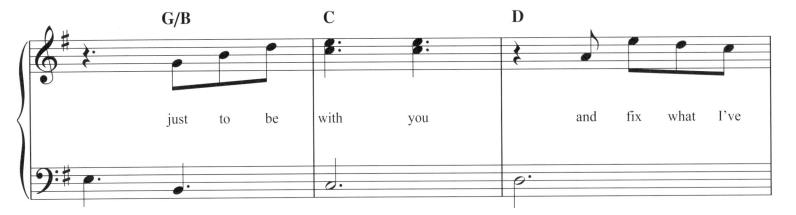

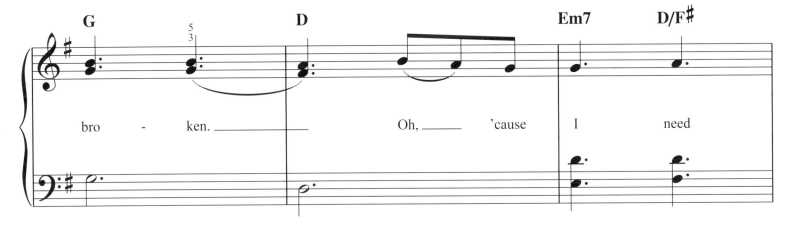

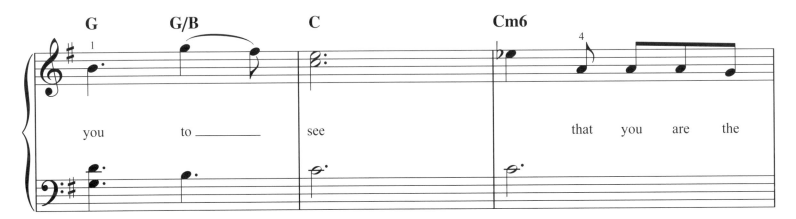

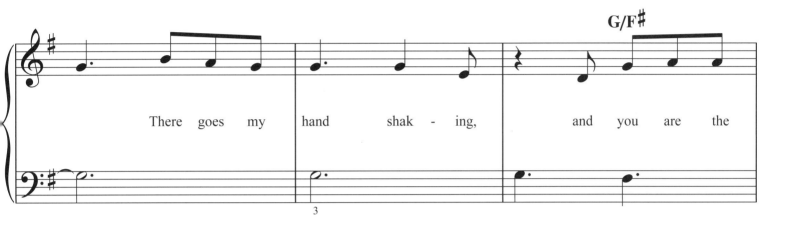

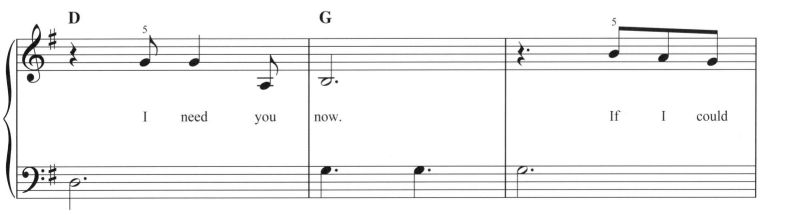

turn   back   the   clock,   I'd   make   sure   the   light   de - feat - ed   the

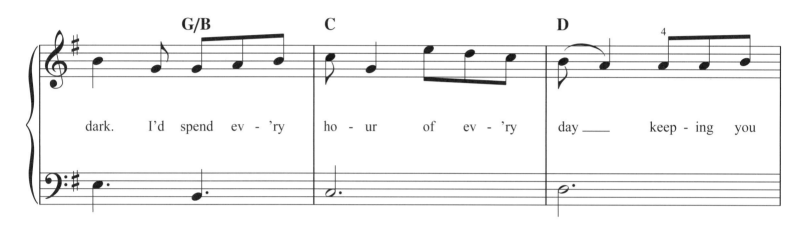

dark.   I'd   spend   ev - 'ry   ho - ur   of   ev - 'ry   day ____   keep - ing   you

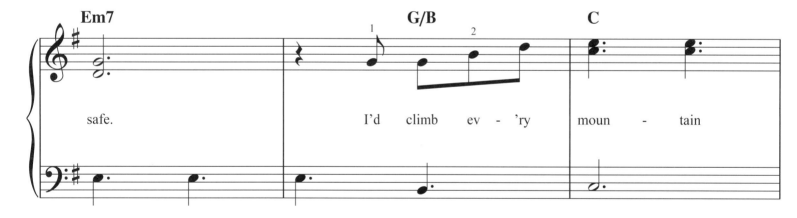

safe.   I'd   climb   ev - 'ry   moun - tain

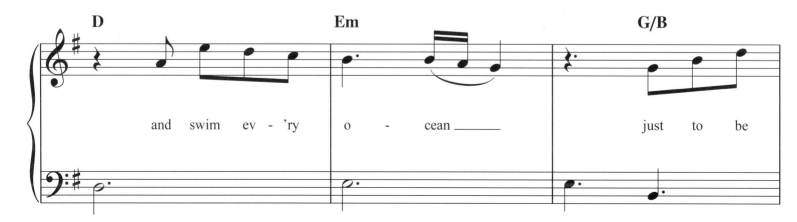

and   swim   ev - 'ry   o - cean ____   just   to   be

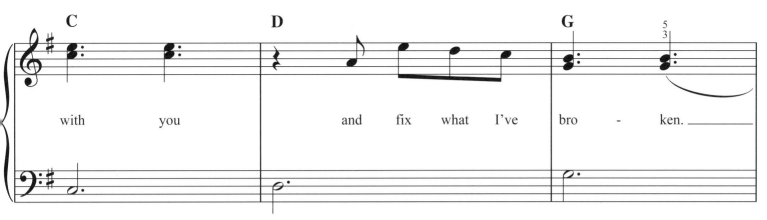

with you — and fix what I've bro - ken. _____

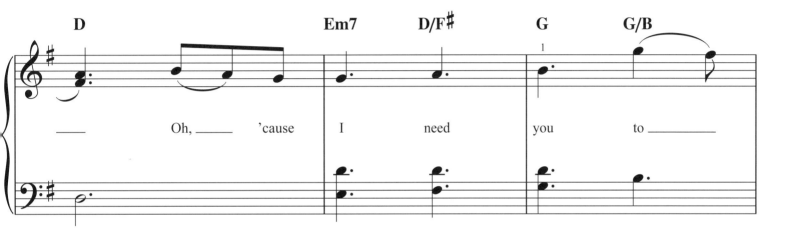

_____ Oh, _____ 'cause I need you to _____

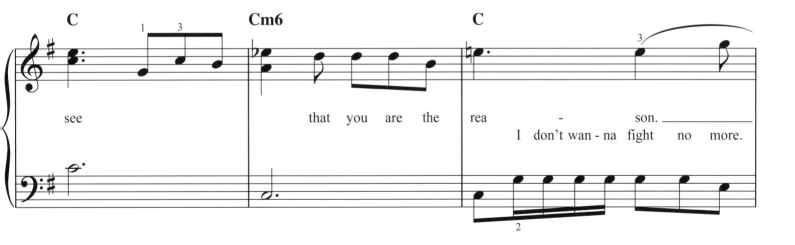

see that you are the rea - son. _____ I don't wan - na fight no more.

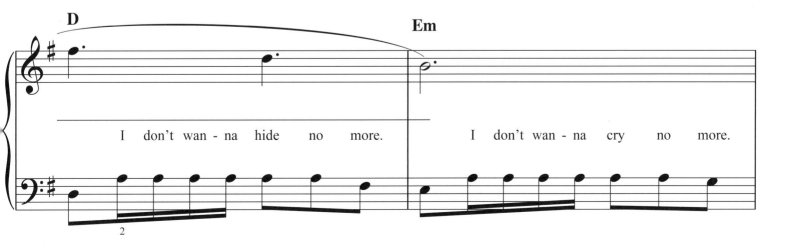

I don't wan - na hide no more. I don't wan - na cry no more.

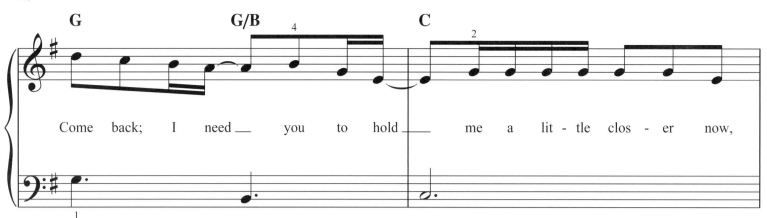

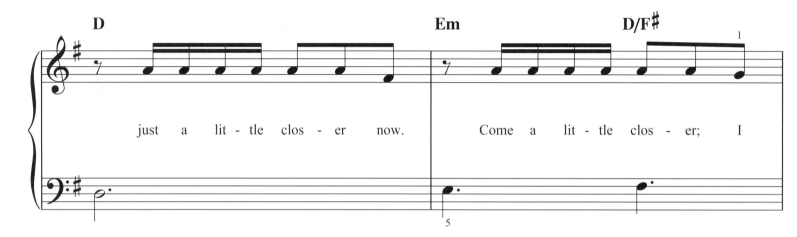

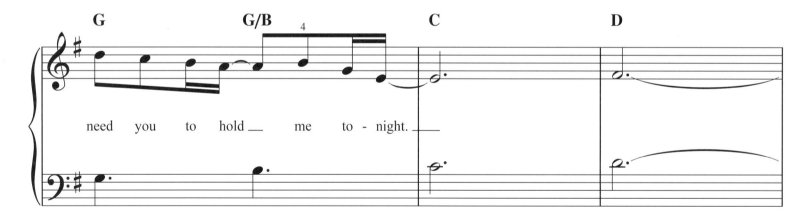

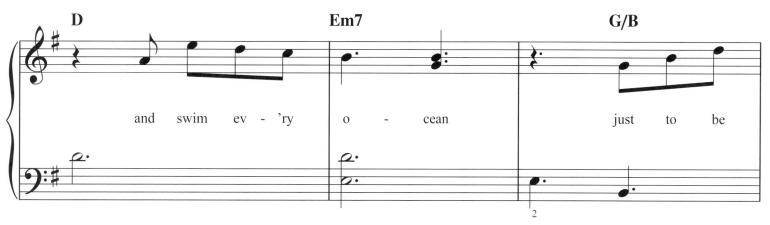

and swim ev - 'ry o - cean just to be

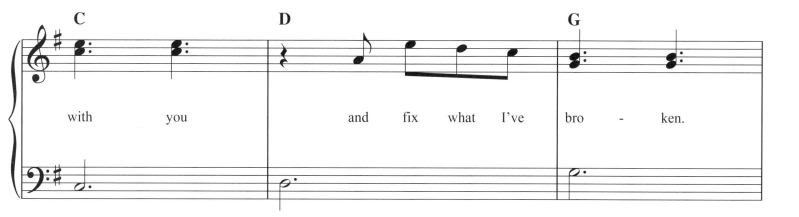

with you and fix what I've bro - ken.

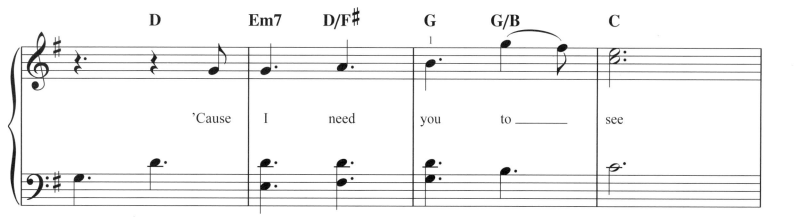

'Cause I need you to _____ see

that you are the rea - son. _____

YOU SAY

Words and Music by LAUREN DAIGLE,
JASON INGRAM and PAUL MABURY

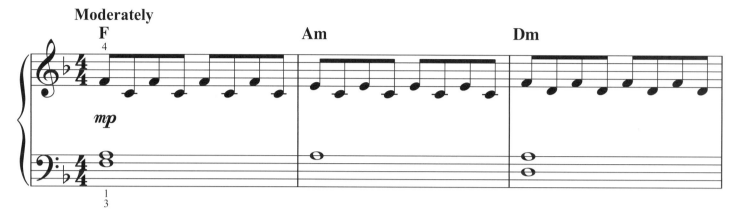

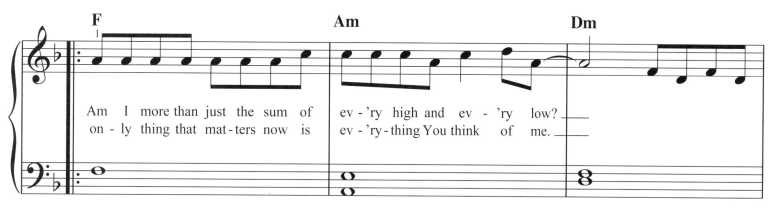

Am I more than just the sum of ev-'ry high and ev-'ry low?
on - ly thing that mat-ters now is ev-'ry-thing You think of me.

Re -mind me once a - gain just who I am, be-cause I need to know.
In You I find my worth, in You I find __ my i - den - ti - ty.

Ooh, oh. You say I am loved when I can't feel a

mf

thing. You say I am strong when I think I am weak. And You say I am held when I am fall-ing

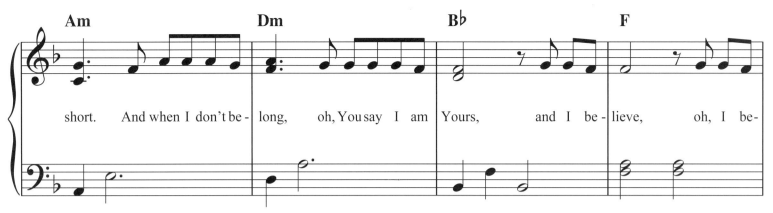

short. And when I don't be - long, oh, You say I am Yours, and I be - lieve, oh, I be-

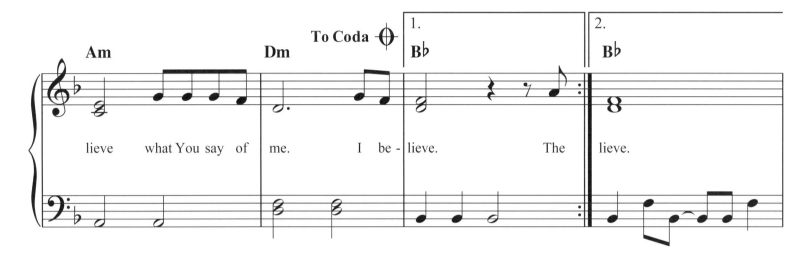

lieve what You say of me. I be - lieve. The lieve.

Tak - ing all I have, and now I'm lay - ing it at Your feet.

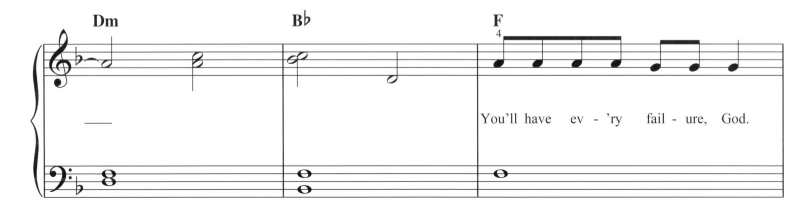

You'll have ev - 'ry fail - ure, God.

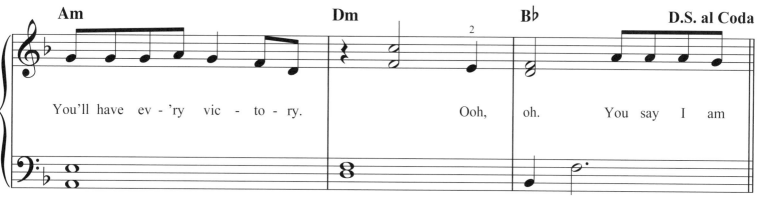

POP PIANO HITS

Pop Piano Hits is a series designed for students of all ages. Each book contains five simple and easy-to-read arrangements of today's most popular downloads. Lyrics, fingering and chord symbols are included to help you make the most of each arrangement. Enjoy your favorite songs and artists today!

BELIEVER, WHAT ABOUT US & MORE HOT SINGLES
Attention (Charlie Puth) • Believer (Imagine Dragons) • There's Nothing Holdin' Me Back (Shawn Mendes) • Too Good at Goodbyes (Sam Smith) • What About Us (P!nk).
00251934 Easy Piano..................$9.99

BLANK SPACE, I REALLY LIKE YOU & MORE HOT SINGLES
Blank Space (Taylor Swift) • Heartbeat Song (Kelly Clarkson) • I Really Like You (Carly Rae Jepsen) • I'm Not the Only One (Sam Smith) • Thinking Out Loud (Ed Sheeran).
00146286 Easy Piano..................$9.99

CAN'T STOP THE FEELING, 7 YEARS & MORE HOT SINGLES
Can't Stop the Feeling (Justin Timberlake) • H.O.L.Y. (Florida Georgia Line) • Just Like Fire (Pink) • Lost Boy (Ruth B.) • 7 Years (Lukas Graham).
00193755 Easy Piano..................$9.99

CITY OF STARS, MERCY & MORE HOT SINGLES
City of Stars (from *La La Land*) • Evermore (from Beauty and the Beast) • Mercy (Shawn Mendes) • Perfect (Ed Sheeran) • Stay (Zedd & Alessia Cara).
00236097 Easy Piano..................$9.99

FEEL IT STILL, REWRITE THE STARS & MORE HOT SINGLES
Feel It Still (Portugal. The Man) • Lost in Japan (Shawn Mendes) • The Middle (Zedd, Maren Morris & Grey) • Rewrite the Stars (from *The Greatest Showman*) • Whatever It Takes (Imagine Dragons).
00278090 Easy Piano..................$9.99

GIRLS LIKE YOU, HAPPY NOW & MORE HOT SINGLES
Girls Like You (Maroon 5) • Happy Now (Zedd feat. Elley Duhé) • Treat Myself (Meghan Trainor) • You Are the Reason (Calum Scott) • You Say (Lauren Daigle).
00285014 Easy Piano..................$9.99

HELLO, BETTER WHEN I'M DANCIN' & MORE HOT SINGLES
Better When I'm Dancin' (Meghan Trainor) • Burning House (Cam) • Drag Me Down (One Direction) • Hello (Adele) • She Used to Be Mine (Sara Bareilles).
00156235 Easy Piano..................$9.99

HOW FAR I'LL GO, THIS TOWN & MORE HOT SINGLES
How Far I'll Go (Alessia Cara - from *Moana*) • My Way (Calvin Harris) • This Town (Niall Horan) • Treat You Better (Shawn Mendes) • We Don't Talk Anymore (Charlie Puth feat. Selena Gomez).
00211286 Easy Piano..................$9.99

LET IT GO, HAPPY & MORE HOT SINGLES
All of Me (John Legend) • Dark Horse (Katy Perry) • Happy (Pharrell) • Let It Go (Demi Lovato) • Pompeii (Bastille).
00128204 Easy Piano..................$9.99

LOVE YOURSELF, STITCHES & MORE HOT SINGLES
Like I'm Gonna Lose You (Meghan Trainor) • Love Yourself (Justin Bieber) • One Call Away (Charlie Puth) • Stitches (Shawn Mendes) • Stressed Out (Twenty One Pilots).
00159285 Easy Piano..................$9.99

ROAR, ROYALS & MORE HOT SINGLES
Atlas (Coldplay – from *The Hunger Games: Catching Fire*) • Roar (Katy Perry) • Royals (Lorde) • Safe and Sound (Capital Cities) • Wake Me Up! (Avicii).
00123868 Easy Piano..................$9.99

SAY SOMETHING, COUNTING STARS & MORE HOT SINGLES
Counting Stars (One Republic) • Demons (Imagine Dragons) • Let Her Go (Passenger) • Say Something (A Great Big World) • Story of My Life (One Direction).
00125356 Easy Piano..................$9.99

SEE YOU AGAIN, FLASHLIGHT & MORE HOT SINGLES
Budapest (George Ezra) • Flashlight (Jessie J.) • Honey I'm Good (Andy Grammer) • See You Again (Wiz Khalifa) • Shut Up and Dance (Walk the Moon).
00150045 Easy Piano..................$9.99

SHAKE IT OFF, ALL ABOUT THAT BASS & MORE HOT SINGLES
All About That Bass (Meghan Trainor) • Shake It Off (Taylor Swift) • A Sky Full of Stars (Coldplay) • Something in the Water (Carrie Underwood) • Take Me to Church (Hozier).
00142734 Easy Piano..................$9.99

HAL•LEONARD®

Prices, contents and availability subject to change without notice.

www.halleonard.com